SWU-800-017

Das Deutsche Heer des Kaiserreiches zur Jahrhundertwende 1871-1918
band 2

LUCA STEFANO CRISTINI
ILLUSTRATIONEN VON R.KNOTEL

Deutsche & English text

SOLDIERSHOP PUBLISHING

AUTHORS

Richard Knötel (January 12, 1857 – April 26, 1914) was one of the most important German artist and pioneer of the study of military uniform. was born in Glogau in 1857. His father, August Knötel, was an art teacher and gave him lessons in drawing and painting from an early age. In this time, Knötel developed an interest in military fashion and history. By late adolescence, he was already employed as an illustrator for the graphics-based newspaper; Illustrierte Zeitung, as well as for postcards and magazines. In 1880, with an established reputation, Knötel was entered into the Berlin Academy of Fine Arts. After his studies, he began collecting books concerning European military history (it is believed that by his death he owned over 9000 titles), and began work on his most famous piece; Uniformenkunde, a huge collection of plates concerning the armies of Europe from the 17th century to 1914. Uniformenkunde is still perhaps the most widely referenced piece of work the study of military attire of the early modern era, and is still used as a source today. As well as an illustrator, Knötel was a talented painter, who was renowned throughout Germany for his military subjects. He died in Berlin in 1914, and is buried in Saint Matthew's Cemetery in the city.

Luca Stefano Cristini born 21 May 1958 in Bergamo (North Italy) It is the author of several titles in Soldiershop series.

PUBLISHING'S NOTE

None of **unpublished** images or text of our book may be reproduced in any format without the expressed written permission of Soldiershop.com when not indicate as marked with license creative commons 3.0 or 4.0. The publisher remains to disposition of the possible having right for all the doubtful sources images or not identifies. Our trademark: Soldiershop Publishing ©, The names of our series: Soldiers&Weapons, Battlefield, War in colour, PaperSoldiers, Soldiershop e-book etc. are herein © by Soldiershop.com.

NOTE ABOUT BOOK PRINTING BEFORE 1925

This book may contain text or images coming from a reproduction of a book published before 1925 (over seventy years ago). No effort has been made to modernize or standardize the spelling used in the original text, so this book may have occasional imperfections such as missing or blurred pages, poor pictures, errant marks, etc. that were either part of the original artifact, or were introduced by the scanning process. We believe this work is culturally important, and despite the imperfections, have elected to bring it back into print (digital and/or paper) as part of our continuing commitment to the preservation of printed works worldwide. We appreciate your understanding of the imperfections in the preservation process, and hope you enjoy this valuable book. Now this book is purpose re-built and is proof-read and re-type set from the original to provide an outstanding experience of reflowing text, also for an ebook reader. However Soldiershop publishing added, enriched, revised and overhauled the text, images, etc. of the cover and the book. Therefore, the job is now to all intents and purposes a derivative work, and the added, new and original parts of the book are the copyright of Soldiershop. On this second unpublished part of the book none of images or text may be reproduced in any format without the expressed written permission of Soldiershop. Almost many of the images of our books and prints are taken from original first edition prints or books that are no longer in copyright and are therefore public domain. We have been a specialized bookstore for a long time so we (and several friends antiquarian booksellers) have readily available a lot of ancient, historical and illustrated books not in copyright. Each of our prints, art designs or illustrations is either our own creation, or a fully digitally restoration by our computer artists, or non copyrighted images. All of our prints are "tagged" with a registered digital copyright. Soldiershop remains to disposition of the possible having right for all the doubtful sources images or not identifies.

LICENSES COMMONS

This book may utilize material marked with license creative commons 3.0 or 4.0 (CC BY 4.0), (CC BY-ND 4.0), (CC BY-SA 4.0) or (CC0 1.0). We give appropriate attribution credit and indicate if change were made below in the acknowledgements field.

ACKNOWLEDGEMENTS

A Special Thanks to NYPL and other institutions for their kindly permission to use some images of his archives, collections or books used in our book.

Title: DAS DEUTSCHE HEER DES KAISERREICHES ZUR JAHRHUNDERTWENDE 18171-1918 - BAND 2
By Luca S. Cristini. Plates by Richard Knötel. First edition by Soldiershop. April 2020
Cover & Art Design: Luca S. Cristini. ISBN code: 978-88-93275699
Published by Luca Cristini Editore, via Orio 35/4- 24050 Zanica (BG) ITALY. www.soldiershop.com

DAS DEUTSCHE HEER DES KAISERREICHES ZUR JAHRHUNDERTWENDE 1871-1918

BAND 2

IV, V, VI, VII UND VIII ARMEE-KORPS

LUCA STEFANO CRISTINI

ILLUSTRATIONEN VON R. KNÖTEL

*

SWU-800-017

Deutsche kaiserfamilie

DEUTSCHES HEER (DEUTSCHES KAISERREICH)

Deutsches Heer war die offizielle Bezeichnung der Landstreitkräfte des Deutschen Kaiserreiches von 1871 bis 1918. Die Verfassung des Deutschen Reiches verwendet daneben noch den Begriff „Reichsheer" in Anlehnung an das Bundesheer des Norddeutschen Bundes.

Oberbefehlshaber des Deutschen Heeres war der Kaiser. Die Truppenkontingente der deutschen Bundesstaaten standen aufgrund von Militärkonventionen unter preußischem Kommando oder waren ins preußische Heer eingegliedert. Ausnahmen waren die Heere der Königreiche Bayern, Sachsen und Württemberg. Diese Staaten hatten sich beim Beitritt zum Norddeutschen Bund sogenannte Reservatrechte ausgehandelt oder entsprechende Regelungen mit Preußen vereinbart. Das bayerische, sächsische und das württembergische Heer stand im Frieden unter dem Befehl seines jeweiligen Landesherrn. Ihre Verwaltung unterstand eigenen Kriegsministerien. Das sächsische und das württembergische Heer bildeten jeweils ein in sich geschlossenes Armeekorps innerhalb des deutschen Heeres. Das bayerische Heer stellte drei eigene Armeekorps und stand bei der Nummerierung der Truppenteile außerhalb der Zählung des restlichen Heeres. Die Kontingente der kleineren deutschen Staaten bildeten in der Regel geschlossene Verbände innerhalb des preußischen Heeres. Württemberg stellte zu Ausbildungszwecken Offiziere zum preußischen Heer ab. Lediglich Bayern verfügte neben Preußen über eine eigene Kriegsakademie. Die Trennung nach Herkunftsstaaten wurde unter den Notwendigkeiten des Ersten Weltkrieges zwar gelockert, aber nicht aufgegeben.

Der Kaiser hatte auch im Frieden das Recht, die Präsenzstärke festzulegen, die Garnisonen zu bestimmen, Festungen anzulegen und für einheitliche Organisation und Formation, Bewaffnung und Kommando sowie Ausbildung der Mannschaften und Qualifikation der Offiziere zu sorgen. Das Militärbudget wurde durch die Parlamente der einzelnen Bundesstaaten festgelegt. Als Streitkräfte außerhalb des Heeres standen die Schutztruppen der deutschen Kolonien und Schutzgebiete und die Marine einschließlich ihrer drei Seebataillone unter direktem Oberbefehl des Kaisers und der Verwaltung des Reichs.

The Imperial German Army (German: Deutsches Heer) was the unified ground and air force of the German Empire (excluding the maritime aviation formations of the Imperial German Navy). The term Deutsches Heer is also used for the modern German Army, the land component of the Bundeswehr. The German Army was formed after the unification of Germany under Prussian leadership in 1871 and dissolved in 1919, after the defeat of the German Empire in World War I. The states that made up the German Empire contributed their armies; within the German Confederation, formed after the Napoleonic Wars, each state was responsible for maintaining certain units to be put at the disposal of the Confederation in case of conflict. When operating together, the units were known as the Federal Army (Bundesheer). The Federal Army system functioned during various conflicts of the 19th century, such as the First Schleswig War from 1848–50 but by the time of the Second Schleswig War of 1864, tension had grown between the main powers of the confederation, the Austrian Empire and the Kingdom of Prussia and the German Confederation was dissolved after the Austro-Prussian War of 1866. Prussia formed the North German Confederation and the treaty provided for the maintenance of a Federal Army and a Federal Navy (Bundesmarine or Bundeskriegsmarine). Further laws on military duty also used these terms.[2] Conventions (some later amended) were entered into between the North German Confederation and its member states, subordinating their armies to the Prussian army in time of war, and giving the Prussian Army control over training, doctrine and equipment. Shortly after the outbreak of the Franco-Prussian War in 1870, the North German Confederation also entered into conventions on military matters with states that were not members of the confederation, namely Bavaria, Württemberg, and Baden.[b] Through these conventions and the 1871 Constitution of the German Empire, an Army of the Realm (Reichsheer) was created. The contingents of the Bavarian, Saxon and Württemberg kingdoms remained semi-autonomous, while the Prussian Army assumed almost total control over the armies of the other states of the Empire. The Constitution of the German Empire, dated April 16, 1871, changed references in the North German Constitution from Federal Army to either Army of the Realm (Reichsheer) or German Army (Deutsches Heer).

INHALT

*

Deutsches Heer (Deutsches Kaiserreich) 5

Bewaffnung und Ausrüstung und uniform 7

TAFELBAND

IV Armee-Korps (Preussen) 13

V Armee-Korps (Preussen) 25

VI Armee-Korps (Preussen) 41

VII Armee-Korps (Preussen) 57

VIII Armee-Korps (Preussen) 71

BEWAFFNUNG UND AUSRÜSTUNG UND UNIFORM

Die Bewaffnung der Infanterie bestand aus dem Gewehr 88, später Gewehr 98, beide für die Patrone 7,92 × 57 mm; das Gewehr 88 bewährte sich nicht und wurde relativ schnell durch die leistungsfähigere Konstruktion des Gewehrs 98 ersetzt, dessen Nachfolger in der Karabiner-Version als Hauptordonenzwaffe Karabiner 98k im Zweiten Weltkrieg geführt wurde, und dem Seitengewehr. Portepee-Unteroffiziere hatten den sogenannten Reichsrevolver und das Offizier-Seitengewehr. Jäger trugen statt des Seitengewehres einen Hirschfänger. Hintergelagerte und spezialisierte Truppenteile zu Fuß wurde erst mit einer verkürzten Versionen des Gewehr 88 ausgerüstet, dies war das Gewehr 91. Später wurde dieses durch eine verkürzte Versionen des Gewehr 98 ersetzte, dem Karabiner 98 Artillerie. Um eine einheitliche kurze Waffe für berittene und unberittene Truppen zu schaffen, wurde mit dem Karabiner 98A ein Einheitskarabiner geschaffen. Da der Karabiner 98A wegen seines kurzen Laufes ein enormes Mündungsfeuer erzeugte, wurde mit dem Karabiner 98AZ eine verlängerte Version geschaffen. Der Kar98AZ wurde vor allem bei den Sturmtruppen im Ersten Weltkrieg verwendet und später in der Reichswehr in Karabiner 98a (klein a) umbenannt.

Bei der Kavallerie gab es statt des Gewehres den Karabiner 88 bzw. Karabiner 98 Kavallerie und Degen, Portepee-Unteroffiziere trugen stattdessen den Offizierssäbel. Dazu wurde auch noch die Lanze geführt. Der Karabiner 88 war eine gekürzte Version des Gewehr 88 und erhielt, aufgrund seines Ganzschaftes den Namen Komissionsstutzen. Wegen des Probleme des 88-Systems wurde mit dem Karabiner 98 Kavallerie eine Karabinerversion des Gewehr 98 eingeführt. Später wurde mit dem Karabiner 98A eine einheitliche kurze Version für Infanterie und Kavallerie geschaffen.

UNIFORM

Zwar wurden die unterschiedlichen Kontingente des Heeres nach der Reichsgründung sukzessive nach einheitlichen Vorgaben ausgestattet, doch folgte man bei Kopfbedeckung sowie Farbgebung und Schnitt dem Grundsatz der Vielfalt in der Einheitlichkeit.

Unterscheidungsmerkmale waren:

Abzeichenfarbe und Knopffarbe (nach dieser richtete sich in der Regel auch die Farbe der Tressen, Litzen, Helmbeschläge)
- Achselklappen (Mannschaften und Unteroffiziere), Schulterstücke (Offiziere) und Epauletten
- Form und Beschläge der Helme
- Kokarden
- Ärmelaufschläge

Beispiele:

INFANTERIE

Der Waffenrock war einreihig mit acht Knöpfen. Die Hosen waren schwarz, im Sommer wurden auch weiße Hosen getragen. Stiefel waren die sogenannten „Knobelbecher".

Der Waffenrock der Infanterie war dunkelblau, der der Jäger und Schützen dunkelgrün. Als einziger Verband der Linieninfanterie trug das Schützen-(Füsilier-)Regiment „Prinz Georg" (Königlich Sächsisches) Nr. 108 grüne Waffenröcke. Die bayerische Infanterie und auch die Jäger trugen hellblaue Waffenröcke. Die Maschinengewehr-Abteilungen trugen graugrüne Waffenröcke.

Der deutsche Soldat bekam einmal im Jahr eine neue Uniform, insgesamt gab es bis zu fünf Garnituren. Die erste Garnitur wurde zur Parade angelegt, die zweite als Ausgehuniform, die dritte und vierte Garnitur zum täglichen Dienst und die fünfte Garnitur, sofern vorhanden, lag für den Kriegsfall in der Kammer.

Die Kontingente der meisten deutschen Staaten waren bereits durch Militärkonventionen in der preußischen Armee aufgegangen oder ihr angegliedert und hatten nur noch kleine Reservatrechte, so den Anspruch auf eigene Kokarden an den Kopfbedeckungen, der unterschiedlichen Helmzier und sonstige Unterscheidungsmerkmale. Zu welchem Kontingent ein Soldat gehörte, konnte an der Landeskokarde der Kopfbedeckung, den Ärmelaufschlägen und den Schulterklappen erkannt werden. Im Jahre 1914 existierten insgesamt 272 verschiedene Variationen in der Uniformierung. Es handelte sich dabei zum Teil nur um Kleinigkeiten (zum Beispiel hatte einzig das Hessische Leibgarde-Infanterie-Regiment Nr. 115 die Knopfleisten der Gardelitzen nicht in der Grundfarbe der Ärmelaufschläge, sondern in Weiß unterlegt. Die fünf hessischen Infanterie-Regimenter trugen auf den Ärmelpatten nicht die Farbe ihres (XVIII.) Armeekorps, sondern jedes Regiment hatte eine andere Farbe, die jedoch eifersüchtig beachtet wurden). Die Landesfarben tauchten auch noch in anderen Bekleidungsstücken und Abzeichen auf, wie beispielsweise Schulterstücken, Feldbinden, Portepees, Einjährigenschnüren und den Auszeichnungsknöpfen für Unteroffiziere und Gefreite.

Sachsen hatte insbesondere folgende Abweichungen: die Schulterklappen waren eckig, der Vorstoß an der Vorderseite des Rockes wurde um die unteren Schoßkanten des Rockes herumgeführt.

Die grundsätzliche Kopfbedeckung war die bekannte „Pickelhaube". Jäger, Schützen und MG-Abteilungen trugen einen Tschako. Zur Parade die zwei preußischen Garderegimenter Grenadiermützen in altpreußischem Stil. Für manche Anzugarten war die Schirmmütze oder für Mannschaften auch das „Krätzchen" (Mütze ohne Schirm) befohlen.

Die Uniformen blieben bis zum Kriegsausbruch weitgehend unverändert. Ab 1897 wurde neben der Landeskokarde nun auch die Reichskokarde getragen.

1907 wurde versuchsweise die erste feldgraue Uniform eingeführt, die nur im Kriegsfalle angelegt werden sollte, aber bereits seit 1909/1910 bei Manövern verwendet wurde. Bis zum Kriegsbeginn und während des Krieges erfuhr die feldgraue Uniform noch einige Änderungen; so wurde die Farbe beispielsweise eher graugrün, der Name „Feldgrau" aber beibehalten. Im Weltkrieg wurde ausschließlich diese „feldgraue" Uniform getragen, anfangs die „Pickelhaube" mit Überzug, ab Mitte des Krieges wurde flächendeckend der Stahlhelm M1916 eingeführt.

KAVALLERIE

Die Kürassiere trugen einen Koller aus weißem Kirsey mit gleichfarbigem Kragen und Schulterklappen, je nach Regiment mit verschiedenenfarbigen Ärmelaufschlägen, Borten, Vorstößen und Kragenpatten. Kopfbedeckung der Kürassiere war eine Pickelhaube mit metallener Glocke, deren Nackenschirm tief nach hinten gezogen war.

Die Schweren Reiter, zu denen man die Kürassiere in Sachsen 1876 und in Bayern 1879 umgewandelt hatte, trugen kornblumenblaue Koller (Sachsen) bzw. Waffenröcke. Während die Sachsen den preußischen Kürassierhelm führten, trugen die Bayern den Lederhelm für Berittene.

Die Ulanen trugen eine dunkelblauem (in Sachsen hellblaue, in Bayern dunkelgrüne) Ulanka mit Epauletten und je abzeichenfarbigen Kragen, Aufschlägen und Vorstößen. Als Kopfbedeckung wurde eine Tschapka getragen.

Die Dragoner trugen einen kornblumenblauem (in Hessen: dunkelgrünen) Waffenrock mit abzeichenfarbigen Kragen, Aufschlägen und Schulterklappen. Helm für Berittene mit Spitze (ähnlich dem der Infanterie).

Die Uniform der nur in Bayern vorhandenen Chevaulegers ähnelte derjenigen der Ulanen, war jedoch dunkelgrün und hatte eckige Schulterklappen und lederne Pickelhauben.

Die Husaren trugen eine Attila in Regimentsfarben mit Schnurbesatz und Achselschnüren. Als Kopfbedeckung diente der Kolpak. Einige Regimenter trugen dazu Pelz.

Die ab 1901 aufgestellten Jäger zu Pferde trugen Koller und Waffenrock aus graugrünem Tuch. Schulterklappen und Aufschläge waren hellgrün und mit farbigen Paspeln abgesetzt. Die Regimenter Nr. 1 bis Nr. 6 trugen geschwärzte Kürassierhelme und Kürassierstiefel. Bei den Regimentern Nr. 7 bis Nr. 13 waren nur die Offiziere so ausgestattet, die Unteroffiziere und Mannschaften dagegen mit Dragonerhelmen und Dragonerstiefeln ausgerüstet. (Die Nachrüstung mit den Kürassierhelmen erfolgte erst 1915, bis dahin hatten diese Helme noch nicht zur Verfügung gestanden.)

Für den Feldanzug wurden 1909 feldgraue Uniformen eingeführt, bei denen die abzeichenfarbigen Elemente meist nur mehr in der entsprechenden Farbe paspeliert waren. Einige neu aufgestellte Truppenteile wie das Husaren-Regiment Nr. 21 erhielten gar keine bunte Friedensuniform mehr. Die Jäger zu Pferde, die ja ohnehin bereits eine etwas grünlichere tarnfarbene Uniform hatten, behielten diese bei.

Flussübergang.

ARTILLERIE, TRAIN UND TECHNISCHE TRUPPEN

Die Artillerie trug einen dunkelblauen Waffenrock mit schwarzen Abzeichen. Statt der Helmspitze wurde zur Vermeidung von Verletzungen eine Kugel getragen, nur in Bayern trug man auch hier die Spitze. Die Soldaten des Trains hatten dunkelblaue Waffenröcke mit hellblauen Abzeichen und einen Tschako. In Sachsen hatten Artillerie, Pioniere und Train dunkelgrüne Waffenröcke, die Abzeichen waren rot bzw. beim Train hellblau. Pioniere und Eisenbahntruppen trugen die Uniform der Artillerie, jedoch mit weißen statt gelben Knöpfen. Flieger-, Luftschiffer- und Telegraphentruppe trugen die Uniform der Artillerie, jedoch statt des Helms den Tschako.

ARMY ARMAMENT, EQUIPMENT & UNIFORMES (ENGLISH)

The armament of the infantry consisted of rifle 88, later rifle 98, both for the 7.92 × 57 mm cartridge; the 88 rifle did not prove itself and was replaced relatively quickly by the more powerful construction of the 98 rifle, the successor of which was the carbine version, the 98A main gun, and the side rifle. Portepee non-commissioned officers had the so-called Reich Revolver and the officer rifle. Hunters carried a deer catcher instead of the side rifle. Backed up and specialized troops on foot were only equipped with a shortened version of rifle 88, this was rifle 91. Later, this was replaced by a shortened version of rifle 98, the carbine 98 artillery. In order to create a uniform short weapon for mounted and non-mounted troops, the carbine 98A was created as a unit carbine. Since the carabiner 98A generated an enormous muzzle flash due to its short barrel, the extended version of the carabiner 98AZ was created. The Kar98AZ was mainly used by the stormtroopers in World War I and was later renamed Karabiner 98a (small a) in the Reichswehr.

The cavalry had the carbine 88 or carbine 98 cavalry and rapier instead of the rifle, Portepee non-commissioned officers instead carried the officer saber. The lance was also guided. The carbine 88 was a shortened version of the rifle 88 and was given the name of a commission socket due to its whole stock. Because of the problem with the 88 system, a carbine version of the 98 rifle was introduced with the Karabiner 98 cavalry. Later, the Karabiner 98A, a uniform short version for infantry and cavalry, was created.

UNIFORM

Although the different contingents of the army were successively equipped according to uniform specifications after the founding of the empire, the principle of diversity in uniformity was followed with headgear, coloring and cut. Distinguishing features were:

Badge color and button color (usually the color of the braids, braids, helmet fittings)
  Armpits (teams and noncommissioned officers), shoulder boards (officers) and epaulets
  Shape and fittings of the helmets
  Cockades
  Cuffs

INFANTRY

The coat was single-breasted with eight buttons. The pants were black, and white pants were also worn in summer. Boots were the so-called "Knobelbecher".

The coat of arms of the infantry was dark blue, that of the hunters and shooters dark green. The rifle (fusilier) regiment "Prince Georg" (Royal Saxon) No. 108 was the only association of the line infantry to wear green armor skirts. The Bavarian infantry, as well as the hunters, wore light blue skirts. The machine gun departments wore gray-green skirts.

The German soldier was given a new uniform once a year, and there were up to five sets in total. The first set was laid out for the parade, the second set for going out, the third and fourth sets for daily service, and the fifth set, if available, was in the chamber for war.

The contingents of most German states had already been absorbed or affiliated to the Prussian army through military conventions and only had small reservation rights, such as the right to have their own cockades on the headgear, the different helmets and other distinguishing features. Which contingent a soldier belonged to could be recognized from the state cockade of the headgear, the cuffs and the epaulettes. In 1914 there were a total of 272 different variations in the uniform. Some of these were just small things (for example, only the Hessian Life Guards Infantry Regiment No. 115 had the button strips of the Gardelitzen not in the basic color of the sleeve cuffs, but in white. The five Hessian infantry regiments carried on the sleeve flaps not the color of their (XVIII.) Army Corps, but each regiment had a different color, which, however, was jealously observed). The national colors also appeared in other items of clothing and badges, such as shoulder pieces, field bandages, portepees, one-year-old cords and the badges for non-commissioned officers and private individuals.

Saxony in particular had the following deviations: the epaulettes were angular, the push on the front of the skirt was led around the lower lap edges of the skirt.

The basic headgear was the well-known "pimple hood". Hunters, riflemen and machine gun departments wore a shako. The two Prussian guards regiments Grenadier hats in old Prussian style to parade. For some types of suit, the peaked cap or for teams also the "little hat" (cap without peak) was ordered.

The uniforms remained largely unchanged until the outbreak of war. From 1897, the Reichskokarde was also worn alongside the Landeskokarde.

In 1907, the first field-gray uniform was introduced on a trial basis, which was only to be worn in the event of war, but had been used in maneuvers since 1909/1910. Before the war began and during the war, the field-gray uniform underwent some changes; For example, the color was rather gray-green, but the name "field gray" was retained. In the World War only this "field gray" uniform was worn, initially the "pickelhaube" with cover, from the middle of the war the M1916 steel helmet was introduced nationwide.

GERMANY - EMPIRE NAVY AND ARMY UNIFORM

CAVALRY

The cuirassiers wore a koller made of white Kirsey with a collar of the same color and epaulettes, depending on the regiment, with different colored cuffs, braids, flaps and collar flaps. The headgear of the cuirassiers was a pimple hood with a metal bell, the neck umbrella of which was drawn low back.

The heavy riders, to whom the cuirassiers in Saxony in 1876 and in Bavaria in 1879 had been converted, wore cornflower-blue koller (Saxony) or armor skirts. While the Saxons wore the Prussian cuirassier helmet, the Bavarians wore the leather helmet for mounted horses.

The Uhlans wore a dark blue (light blue in Saxony, dark green in Bavaria) ulanka with epaulettes and badge-colored collars, cuffs and advances. A chapka was worn as headgear.

The Dragoons wore a cornflower blue (in Hessen: dark green) tunic with a badge-colored collar, cuffs and epaulettes. Helmet for mounted with a tip (similar to that of the infantry).

The uniform of the Chevaulegers only available in Bavaria was similar to that of the Uhlans, but was dark green and had angular epaulettes and leather pimples.

The hussars wore an Attila in regimental colors with cord trim and armpit cords. The Kolpak served as headgear. Some regiments wore fur.

The hunters on horseback, set up in 1901, wore koller and tunic made of gray-green cloth. Epaulets and cuffs were light green and trimmed with colored piping. Regiments No. 1 to No. 6 wore blackened cuirassier helmets and cuirassier boots. Regiments No. 7 to No. 13 were only equipped with officers, while non-commissioned officers and men were equipped with dragoon helmets and boots. (The retrofitting with cuirassier helmets only took place in 1915, until then these helmets had not been available.)

For the field suit, field-gray uniforms were introduced in 1909, in which the badge-colored elements were mostly only piped in the appropriate color. Some newly formed troops, such as the Hussar Regiment No. 21, no longer received a colorful peace uniform. The hunters on horseback, who already had a slightly greener camouflage-colored uniform, kept it.

ARTILLERY, TRAIN AND TECHNICAL TROOPS

The artillery was wearing a dark blue tunic with black markings. Instead of the helmet tip, a ball was worn to avoid injuries, only in Bavaria was the tip worn. The soldiers of the train had dark blue skirts with light blue markings and a shako. In Saxony, artillery, pioneers and Train had dark green skirts, the badges were red and the Train light blue. Pioneers and railway troops wore the uniform of the artillery, but with white instead of yellow buttons. Aviation, airship and telegraph troops wore the artillery uniform, but the shako instead of the helmet.

IV ARMEE-KORPS (PREUSSEN)

7. Division in Magdeburg
8. Division in Halle (Saale)
Magdeburgisches Jäger-Bataillon Nr. 4 in Naumburg (Saale)
Fußartillerie-Regiment „Encke" (Magdeburgisches) Nr. 4 in Magdeburg
Magdeburgisches Pionier-Bataillon Nr. 4 in Magdeburg
Magdeburgisches Train-Bataillon Nr. 4 in Magdeburg

7 division

13. Infanterie-Brigade in Magdeburg
  Infanterie-Regiment „Fürst Leopold von Anhalt-Dessau" (1. Magdeburgisches) Nr. 26 in Magdeburg
  3. Magdeburgisches Infanterie-Regiment Nr. 66 in Magdeburg
14. Infanterie-Brigade in Halberstadt
  Infanterie-Regiment „Prinz Louis Ferdinand von Preußen" (2. Magdeburgisches) Nr. 27 in Halberstadt
  5. Hannoversches Infanterie-Regiment Nr. 165 in Quedlinburg und Blankenburg (II.Bataillon)
7. Kavallerie-Brigade in Magdeburg
  Magdeburgisches Husaren-Regiment Nr. 10 in Stendal
  Ulanen-Regiment „Hennigs von Treffenfeld" (Altmärkisches) Nr. 16 in Salzwedel und Gardelegen (2. und 5. Eskadron)
7. Feldartillerie-Brigade in Magdeburg
  Feldartillerie-Regiment „Prinzregent Luitpold von Bayern" (Magdeburgisches) Nr. 4 in Magdeburg
    Altmärkisches Feldartillerie-Regiment Nr. 40 in Burg

8 division

15. Infanterie-Brigade in Halle (Saale)
  Füsilier-Regiment „General-Feldmarschall Graf Blumenthal" (Magdeburgisches) Nr. 36 in Halle (Saale) und Bernburg (II. Bataillon)
  Anhaltisches Infanterie-Regiment Nr. 93 in Dessau und Zerbst (II. Bataillon)
16. Infanterie-Brigade in Torgau
  4. Thüringisches Infanterie-Regiment Nr. 72 in Torgau und Eilenburg (III. Bataillon)
  8. Thüringisches Infanterie-Regiment Nr. 153 in Altenburg und Merseburg (III. Bataillon)
8. Kavallerie-Brigade in Halle (Saale)
  Kürassier-Regiment „von Seydlitz" (Magdeburgisches) Nr. 7 in Halberstadt und Quedlinburg (1. Eskadron)
  Thüringisches Husaren-Regiment Nr. 12 in Torgau
8. Feldartillerie-Brigade in Halle (Saale)
  Torgauer Feldartillerie-Regiment Nr. 74 in Torgau und Wittenberg (II. Abteilung)
  Mansfelder Feldartillerie-Regiment Nr. 75 in Halle (Saale)
Landwehr-Inspektion Halle (Saale)

7. Division 13. Infanterie-Brigade 3. Magdeburgisches Infanterie-Regiment Nr. 66 in Magdeburg

7. Division 7. Kavallerie brigade Magdeburgisches Husaren-Regiment Nr. 10 in Stendal

7.Division 7. Kavallerie brigade Ulanen-Regiment „Hennigs von Treffenfeld" (Altmärkisches) Nr. 16 in Salzwedel und Gardelegen

7. Division Feldartillerie-Regiment „Prinzregent Luitpold von Bayern" (Magdeburgisches) Nr. 4 in Magdeburg

8.Division 16.Infanterie-Brigade 4.Thüringisches Infanterie-Regiment Nr. 72 in Torgau und Eilenburg (3.Bataillon)

8.Division 16.Infanterie-Brigade 8.Thüringisches Infanterie-Regiment Nr. 153 in Altenburg und Merseburg (3.Bataillon)

8. Division. 8. Kavallerie brigade Kürassier-Regiment „von Seydlitz" (Magdeburgisches) Nr. 7 in Halberstadt und Quedlinburg

8-Division. 8, Kavallerie brigade Thüringisches Husaren-Regiment Nr. 12 in Torgau

Magdeburgisches Pionier-Bataillon Nr. 4 in Magdeburg

Fußartillerie-Regiment „Encke" (Magdeburgisches) Nr. 4 in Magdeburg

Magdeburgisches Train-Bataillon Nr. 4 in Magdeburg

V ARMEE-KORPS (PREUSSEN)

9. Division in Glogau
10. Division in Posen
Jäger-Bataillon „von Neumann" (1. Schlesisches) Nr. 5 in Hirschberg
Festungs-Maschinengewehr-Abteilung Nr. 6 in Posen
Niederschlesisches Fußartillerie-Regiment Nr. 5 in Posen
Kommando der Pioniere des V. Armee-Korps
   Niederschlesisches Pionier-Bataillon Nr. 5 in Glogau
   Posensches Pionier-Bataillon Nr. 29 in Posen
Festungs-Fernsprech-Kompanie Nr. 8 in Posen
Flieger-Bataillon Nr. 2 in Posen, Graudenz und Königsberg i. Pr.
Niederschlesische Train-Abteilung Nr. 5 in Posen

9 division

17. Infanterie-Brigade in Glogau
  Infanterie-Regiment „von Courbière" (2. Posensches) Nr. 19 in Görlitz und Lauban (II. Bataillon)
  3. Posensches Infanterie-Regiment Nr. 58 in Glogau und Fraustadt (III. Bataillon)
18. Infanterie-Brigade in Liegnitz
  Grenadier-Regiment „König Wilhelm I." (2. Westpreußisches) Nr. 7 in Liegnitz
  5. Niederschlesisches Infanterie-Regiment Nr. 154 in Jauer und Striegau (III. Bataillon)
9. Kavallerie-Brigade in Glogau
  Dragoner-Regiment „von Bredow" (1. Schlesisches) Nr. 4 in Lüben
  Ulanen-Regiment „Prinz August von Württemberg" (Posensches) Nr. 10 in Züllichau
9. Feldartillerie-Brigade in Glogau
  Feldartillerie-Regiment „von Podbielski" (1. Niederschlesisches) Nr. 5 in Sprottau und Sagan (Reitende Abteilung)
  2. Niederschlesisches Feldartillerie-Regiment Nr. 41 in Glogau

10 division

19. Infanterie-Brigade in Posen
  Grenadier-Regiment „Graf Kleist von Nollendorf" (1. Westpreußisches) Nr. 6 in Posen
  Infanterie-Regiment „Graf Kirchbach" (1. Niederschlesisches) Nr. 46 in Posen und Wreschen (III. Bataillon)
20. Infanterie-Brigade in Posen
  Infanterie-Regiment „König Ludwig III. von Bayern" (2. Niederschlesisches) Nr. 47 in Posen und Schrimm (II. Bataillon)
  3. Niederschlesisches Infanterie-Regiment Nr. 50 in Rawitsch und Lissa (III. Bataillon)
77. Infanterie-Brigade in Ostrowo
  Füsilier-Regiment „von Steinmetz" (Westpreußisches) Nr. 37 in Krotoschin
  7. Westpreußisches Infanterie-Regiment Nr. 155 in Ostrowo und Pleschen (III. Bataillon)
10. Kavallerie-Brigade in Posen
  Ulanen-Regiment „Kaiser Alexander III. von Rußland" (Westpreußisches) Nr. 1 in Militsch und Ostrowo (3. Eskadron)
  Regiment Königs-Jäger zu Pferde Nr. 1 in Posen
10. Feldartillerie-Brigade in Posen
  1. Posensches Feldartillerie-Regiment Nr. 20 in Posen
  2. Posensches Feldartillerie-Regiment Nr. 56 in Lissa

9. Division 17. Infanterie-Brigade 3. Posensches Infanterie-Regiment Nr. 58 in Glogau und Fraustadt (3. Bataillon)

9.Division 18.Infanterie-Brigade Grenadier-Regiment „König Wilhelm I." (2. Westpreußisches) Nr. 7 in Liegnitz

9.Division 18.Infanterie-Brigade Grenadier-Regiment „König Wilhelm I." (2. Westpreußisches) Nr. 7 in Liegnitz

9.Division Feldartillerie-Regiment „von Podbielski" (1. Niederschlesisches) Nr. 5 in Sprottau und Sagan

9.Division 9.Kavallerie-Brigade Dragoner-Regiment „von Bredow" (1. Schlesisches) Nr. 4 in Lüben

9.Division 9.Kavallerie-Brigade Ulanen-Regiment „Prinz August von Württemberg" (Posensches) Nr. 10 in Züllichau

10. Division 19. Infanterie-Brigade Grenadier-Regiment „Graf Kleist von Nollendorf" (1. Westpreußisches) Nr. 6 in Posen

10.Division 20.Infanterie-Brigade 3. Niederschlesisches Infanterie-Regiment Nr. 50 in Rawitsch und Lissa (3.Bataillon)

10. Division 77. Infanterie-Brigade Füsilier-Regiment „von Steinmetz" (Westpreußisches) Nr. 37 in Krotoschin

10.Division 10.Kavallerie-Brigade Ulanen-Regiment „Kaiser Alexander 3 von Rußland" (Westpreußisches) Nr. 1 in Militsch und Ostrowo

Niederschlesisches Fußartillerie-Regiment Nr. 5 in Posen

Niederschlesische Train-Abteilung Nr. 5 in Posen

Niederschlesisches Pionier-Bataillon Nr. 5 in Glogau

Flieger-Bataillon Nr. 2 in Posen, Graudenz und Königsberg i. Pr.

Jäger-Bataillon „von Neumann" (1. Schlesisches) Nr. 5 in Hirschberg

VI ARMEE-KORPS (PREUSSEN)

11. Division in Breslau
12. Division in Neiße
2. Schlesisches Jäger-Bataillon Nr. 6 in Oels
Maschinengewehr-Abteilung Nr. 1 in Breslau
Fußartillerie-Regiment „von Dieskau" (Schlesisches) Nr. 6 in Neiße und Glogau
Schlesisches Pionier-Bataillon Nr. 6 in Neiße
Schlesische Train-Abteilung Nr. 6 in Breslau

11 division

21. Infanterie-Brigade in Schweidnitz
  Grenadier-Regiment „König Friedrich Wilhelm II." (1. Schlesisches) Nr. 10 in Schweidnitz
  Füsilier-Regiment „General-Feldmarschall Graf Moltke" (Schlesisches) Nr. 38 in Glatz
22. Infanterie-Brigade in Breslau
  Grenadier-Regiment „König Friedrich III." (2. Schlesisches) Nr. 11 in Breslau
  4. Niederschlesisches Infanterie-Regiment Nr. 51 in Breslau
11. Kavallerie-Brigade in Breslau
  Leib-Kürassier-Regiment „Großer Kurfürst" (Schlesisches) Nr. 1 in Breslau
  Dragoner-Regiment „König Friedrich III." (2. Schlesisches) Nr. 8 in Oels, Kreuzburg in Oberschlesien (2. Eskadron), Bernstadt (3. Eskadron) und Namslau (5. Eskadron)
11. Feldartillerie-Brigade in Breslau
  Feldartillerie-Regiment „von Peucker" (1. Schlesisches) Nr. 6 in Breslau
  2. Schlesisches Feldartillerie-Regiment Nr. 42 in Schweidnitz

12 division

23. Infanterie-Brigade in Gleiwitz
  Infanterie-Regiment „Keith" Nr. 22 (1. Oberschlesisches) in Gleiwitz und Kattowitz (III. Bataillon)
  3. Schlesisches Infanterie-Regiment Nr. 156 in Beuthen in Oberschlesien und Tarnowitz (III. Bataillon)
24. Infanterie-Brigade in Neiße
  Infanterie-Regiment „von Winterfeldt" (2. Oberschlesisches) Nr. 23 in Neiße
  3. Oberschlesisches Infanterie-Regiment Nr. 62 in Cosel und Ratibor (III. Bataillon)
78. Infanterie-Brigade in Brieg
  4. Oberschlesisches Infanterie-Regiment Nr. 63 in Oppeln und Lublinitz (III. Bataillon)
  4. Schlesisches Infanterie-Regiment Nr. 157 in Brieg
12. Kavallerie-Brigade in Neiße
  Husaren-Regiment „von Schill" (1. Schlesisches) Nr. 4 in Ohlau
  Husaren-Regiment „Graf Goetzen" (2. Schlesisches) Nr. 6 in Leobschütz und Ratibor (3. Eskadron)
44. Kavallerie-Brigade in Gleiwitz
  Ulanen-Regiment „von Katzler" (Schlesisches) Nr. 2 in Gleiwitz und Pleß (4. Eskadron)
  Jäger-Regiment zu Pferde Nr. 11 in Tarnowitz und Lublinitz (5. Eskadron)
12. Feldartillerie-Brigade in Neiße
  Feldartillerie-Regiment „von Clausewitz" (1. Oberschlesisches) Nr. 21 in Neiße und Grottkau (II. Abteilung)
  2. Oberschlesisches Feldartillerie-Regiment Nr. 57 in Neustadt in Oberschlesien und Gleiwitz (II. Abteilung)

11.Division 21.Infanterie-Brigade Grenadier-Regiment „König Friedrich Wilhelm II." (1. Schlesisches) Nr. 10 in Schweidnitz

11.Division 22.Infanterie-Brigade Grenadier-Regiment „König Friedrich III." (2. Schlesisches) Nr. 11 in Breslau

11.Division 22.Infanterie-Brigade 4. Niederschlesisches Infanterie-Regiment Nr. 51 in Breslau

11.Division Feldartillerie-Regiment „von Peucker" (1. Schlesisches) Nr. 6 in Breslau

11.Division 11.Kavallerie-Brigade Leib-Kürassier-Regiment „Großer Kurfürst" (Schlesisches) Nr. 1 in Breslau

11.Division 11.Kavallerie-Brigade Dragoner-Regiment „König Friedrich III." (2. Schlesisches) Nr. 8 in Oels, Kreuzburg in Oberschlesien

12.Division 23.Infanterie-Brigade Infanterie-Regiment "Keith" Nr. 22 (1. Oberschlesisches) in Gleiwitz und Kattowitz

12. Division 23. Kavallerie-Brigade 3. Schlesisches Infanterie-Regiment Nr. 156 in Beuthen in Oberschlesien und Tarnowitz

12.Division 12.Kavallerie-Brigade Husaren-Regiment „von Schill" (1. Schlesisches) Nr. 4 in Ohlau

12 Division 12 Kavallerie-Brigade Husaren-Regiment „Graf Goetzen" (2. Schlesisches) Nr. 6 in Leobschütz und Ratibor

12.Division 44.Kavallerie-Brigade Ulanen-Regiment „von Katzler" (Schlesisches) Nr. 2 in Gleiwitz und Pleß

12. Division Feldartillerie-Regiment „von Clausewitz" (1. Oberschlesisches) Nr. 21 in Neiße und Grottkau

Schlesische Train-Abteilung Nr. 6 in Breslau

Schlesisches Pionier-Bataillon Nr. 6 in Neiße

2. Schlesisches Jäger-Bataillon Nr. 6 in Oels

VII ARMEE-KORPS (PREUSSEN)

13. Division in Münster
14. Division in Düsseldorf
Westfälisches Jäger-Bataillon Nr. 7 in Bückeburg
Eskadron Jäger zu Pferde des VII. Armee-Korps (zugeteilt dem 2. Westfälischen Husaren-Regiment Nr. 11) in Wesel
Westfälisches Fußartillerie-Regiment Nr. 7 in Köln
Westfälisches Pionier-Bataillon Nr. 7 in Deutz
Westfälisches Train-Bataillon Nr. 7 in Münster

13 division

25. Infanterie-Brigade in Münster
Infanterie-Regiment „Herwarth von Bittenfeld" (1. Westfälisches) Nr. 13 in Münster
7. Lothringisches Infanterie-Regiment Nr. 158 in Paderborn und Senne
26. Infanterie-Brigade in Minden
Infanterie-Regiment „Prinz Friedrich der Niederlande" (2. Westfälisches) Nr. 15 in Minden
Infanterie-Regiment „Graf Bülow von Dennewitz" (6. Westfälisches) Nr. 55 in Detmold, Höxter und Bielefeld
13. Kavallerie-Brigade in Münster
Kürassier-Regiment „von Driesen" (Westfälisches) Nr. 4 in Münster
Husaren-Regiment „Kaiser Nikolaus II. von Russland" (1. Westfälisches) Nr. 8 in Schloß Neuhaus und Paderborn
13. Feldartillerie-Brigade in Münster
2. Westfälisches Feldartillerie-Regiment Nr. 22 in Münster
Mindensches Feldartillerie-Regiment Nr. 58 in Minden
Landwehr-Inspektion Dortmund

14 division

27. Infanterie-Brigade in Köln
Infanterie-Regiment „Freiherr von Sparr" (3. Westfälisches) Nr. 16 in Köln
5. Westfälisches Infanterie-Regiment Nr. 53 in Köln
28. Infanterie-Brigade in Düsseldorf
Niederrheinisches Füsilier-Regiment Nr. 39 in Düsseldorf
8. Lothringisches Infanterie-Regiment Nr. 159 in Mülheim an der Ruhr und Geldern
79. Infanterie-Brigade in Wesel
Infanterie-Regiment „Vogel von Falckenstein" (7. Westfälisches) Nr. 56 in Wesel und Kleve Infanterie-Regiment „Herzog Ferdinand von Braunschweig" (8. Westfälisches) Nr. 57 in Wesel
14. Kavallerie-Brigade in Düsseldorf
2. Westfälisches Husaren-Regiment Nr. 11 in Krefeld
Westfälisches Ulanen-Regiment Nr. 5 in Düsseldorf
14. Feldartillerie-Brigade in Wesel
1. Westfälisches Feldartillerie-Regiment Nr. 7 in Wesel und Düsseldorf
Klevesches Feldartillerie-Regiment Nr. 43 in Kleve

13.Division 25.Infanterie-Brigade Infanterie-Regiment „Herwarth von Bittenfeld" (1. Westfälisches) Nr. 13 in Münster

13. Division 25. Infanterie-Brigade 7. Lothringisches Infanterie-Regiment Nr. 158 in Paderborn und Senne

13.Division 13.Kavallerie-Brigade Kürassier-Regiment „von Driesen" (Westfälisches) Nr. 4 in Münster

13.Division 13.Kavallerie-Brigade Husaren-Regiment „Kaiser Nikolaus II. von Russland" (1. Westfälisches) Nr. 8 in Schloß Neuhaus und Paderborn

13. Division 13. Feldartillerie-Brigade 2. Westfälisches Feldartillerie-Regiment Nr. 22 in Münster

14. Division 27. Infanterie Brigade 5. Westfälisches Infanterie-Regiment Nr. 53 in Köln

14.Division 79.Infanterie Brigade Infanterie-Regiment „Herzog Ferdinand von Braunschweig" (8. Westfälisches) Nr. 57 in Wesel

14 Division 14 Feldartillerie-Brigade 1. Westfälisches Feldartillerie-Regiment Nr. 7 in Wesel und Düsseldorf

14.Division 14.Kavallerie-Brigade 2. Westfälisches Husaren-Regiment Nr. 11 in Krefeld

14 Division 14 Kavallerie-Brigade Westfälisches Ulanen-Regiment Nr. 5 in Düsseldorf

Westfälisches Jäger-Bataillon Nr. 7 in Bückeburg

Westfälisches Pionier-Bataillon Nr. 7 in Deutz

Westfälisches Train-Bataillon Nr. 7 in Münster

VIII ARMEE-KORPS (PREUSSEN)

15. Division in Köln
16. Division in Trier
Maschinengewehr-Abteilung Nr. 2 in Trier
Festungs-Maschinengewehr-Abteilung Nr. 2 in Köln
Schleswig-Holsteinisches Fußartillerie-Regiment Nr. 9 in Ehrenbreitstein und Köln
Kommando der Pioniere des VIII. Armee-Korps
    1. Rheinisches Pionier-Bataillon Nr. 8 in Ehrenbreitstein
    3. Rheinisches Pionier-Bataillon Nr. 30 in Ehrenbreitstein
Telegraphen-Bataillon Nr. 3 in Koblenz und Darmstadt
Festungs-Fernsprech-Kompanie Nr. 6 in Köln
Luftschiffer-Bataillon Nr. 3 in Köln, Düsseldorf und vorläufig in Metz
Flieger-Bataillon Nr. 3 in Köln, Hannover und Darmstadt
1. Rheinische Train-Abteilung Nr. 8, vorläufig in Ehrenbreitstein

15 division

29. Infanterie-Brigade in Aachen
    Infanterie-Regiment „von Lützow" (1. Rheinisches) Nr. 25 in Aachen
    10. Rheinisches Infanterie-Regiment Nr. 161 in Düren, Eschweiler und Jülich
30. Infanterie-Brigade in Koblenz
    Infanterie-Regiment „von Goeben" (2. Rheinisches) Nr. 28 in Koblenz
    6. Rheinisches Infanterie-Regiment Nr. 68 – Erbgroßherzog-Friedrich-Kaserne in Koblenz
15. Kavallerie-Brigade in Köln
    Kürassier-Regiment „Graf Gessler" (Rheinisches) Nr. 8 in Deutz
    Husaren-Regiment „König Wilhelm I." (1. Rheinisches) Nr. 7 in Bonn
15. Feldartillerie-Brigade in Köln
    Bergisches Feldartillerie-Regiment Nr. 59 in Köln-Riehl
    3. Rheinisches Feldartillerie-Regiment Nr. 83
Landwehrinspektion Köln

16 division

31. Infanterie-Brigade in Trier
    Infanterie-Regiment „von Horn" (3. Rheinisches) Nr. 29 in Trier (Hornkaserne Trier-West/Pallien)
    7. Rheinisches Infanterie-Regiment Nr. 69 in Trier (Agneten-, Goeben-, Maximin- und Palastkaserne)
32. Infanterie-Brigade in Saarbrücken
    8. Rheinisches Infanterie-Regiment Nr. 70 in Saarbrücken
    10. Lothringisches Infanterie-Regiment Nr. 174 in Forbach und Straßburg
80. Infanterie-Brigade in Bonn
    5. Rheinisches Infanterie-Regiment Nr. 65 in Köln
    9. Rheinisches Infanterie-Regiment Nr. 160 in Bonn, Diez und Euskirchen
16. Kavallerie-Brigade in Trier
    Jäger-Regiment zu Pferde Nr. 7 in Trier (Jägerkaserne Trier-Nord)
    Jäger-Regiment zu Pferde Nr. 8 in Trier (Jägerkaserne Trier-West)
16. Feldartillerie-Brigade in Trier
    2. Rheinisches Feldartillerie-Regiment Nr. 23 (Fischel-Kaserne in Koblenz)
    Triersches Feldartillerie-Regiment Nr. 44 in Trier (Artillerie-Kaserne)

15.Division 29.Infanterie-Brigade Infanterie-Regiment „von Lützow" (1. Rheinisches) Nr. 25 in Aachen

15.Division 30.Infanterie-Brigade 6.Rheinisches Infanterie-Regiment Nr. 68 - Erbgroßherzog-Friedrich-Kaserne in Koblenz

15.Division 15.Kavallerie-Brigade Kürassier-Regiment „Graf Gessler" (Rheinisches) Nr. 8 in Deutz

15.Division 15.Kavallerie-Brigade Husaren-Regiment „König Wilhelm I." (1. Rheinisches) Nr. 7 in Bonn

16 Division 80 Infanterie-Brigade 9. Rheinisches Infanterie-Regiment Nr. 160 in Bonn, Diez und Euskirchen

16.Division 2.Rheinisches Feldartillerie-Regiment Nr. 23 (Fischel-Kaserne in Koblenz)

1. Rheinisches Pionier-Bataillon Nr. 8 in Ehrenbreitstein

Schleswig-Holsteinisches Fußartillerie-Regiment Nr. 9 in Ehrenbreitstein und Köln

1. Rheinische Train-Abteilung Nr. 8, vorläufig in Ehrenbreitstein

TITOLI PUBBLICATI - ALREADY PUBLISHING

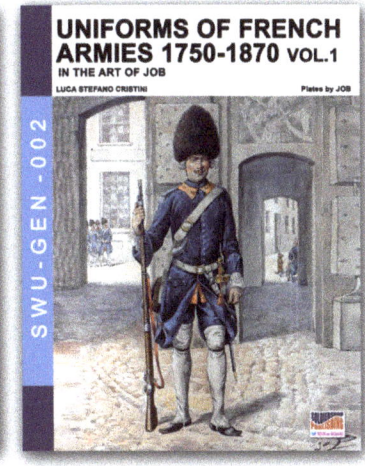
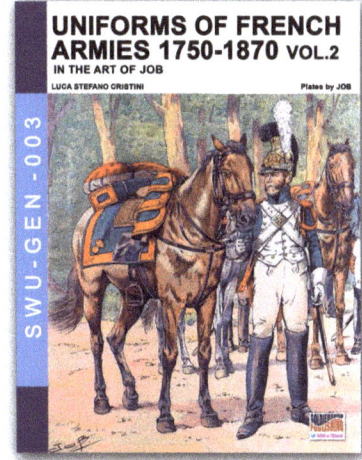
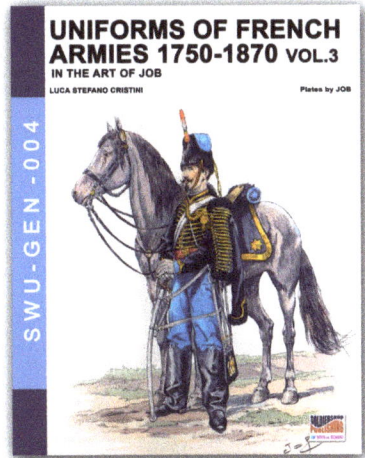

www.ingramcontent.com/pod-product-compliance
Lightning Source LLC
LaVergne TN
LVHW070528070526
838199LV00073B/6727